Proverbs of a Troubled Soul

Curtis C. Greene

Wisdom Is Pain

PROVERBS OF A TROUBLED SOUL
"The Man That Loss His Way"

I was once so well rounded such a brilliant mind full

of many talents. I made progress so fast I clearly loss

my balance. I never was disrespectful before. In

relationships I never treated every woman like whore.

Once I even feared God in my prime. What happened

to the kind man that loved children? What happened

to the friend that loved to bring smiles the lonely?

Now I've become what I feared the most. I'm the self-

righteous idiot that everybody wishes to die. I'm a

master of my craft so my employees play nice and say

hi. The pain I endured on the road to success was a

very lonely and traumatic ride. Nobody dropped by to

see how I was doing when my hard times came.

Nobody had the courtesy to call me up and say hi.

Many days I sat alone in my four corned room and

PROVERBS OF A TROUBLED SOUL

I'll admit I cried. I once reached out to everybody

when I could but nobody reached back when I needed

it so I felt ashamed. Now I kick people when they're

down to keep them down so curses are placed next to

my name. I hate people with a bitter hatred and

there's no remedy for my pain. I hate to look in the

mirror and I hate for people to call my name. I hate

myself and I hate you and I wish I never was born. I

wish I could go back to the days long ago when my

heart was warm. I'm on my death bed now and I

know I've made lite of the chances Jesus gave me for

atonement. Instead of choosing light I chose darkness.

My hateful ways displayed a shameful performance.

Now Satan has sent his reapers to drag me kicking

and screaming to hell. If you lose your grace in

tribulation you will meet the same fate as well.

Matthew 5: 46

For if ye love them which love you what reward have
ye? Do not even the publicans the same?

"Surrounded by Obstacles"

Everywhere I turn the lord sends me a new challenge.

Sometimes I feel like there's no rest for the weary

every day it's more of the same. How many obstacles

shall I overcome before I can live without stress? The

bible says we must study to show ourselves approved

so in that sense I guess I'm blessed. Since I've been

walking a virtuous path for the last six years I've

never known so much trouble. I just want to be in a

real place with God. I sacrificed my personal feelings

and childish dreams for the blessings of the prince of

peace. Though I'm surrounded by obstacles I will lose

my life before I go astray. Though the Lord allows

PROVERBS OF A TROUBLED SOUL

Satan to bruise my heels his petty efforts can't shake

my faith. I chose to become a minister of Christ not

for an extra title but to awaken this world I love.

Though we are surrounded by obstacles our safe place

abides in Christ's love.

Revelation 2: 7

He that hath an ear let him hear what the spirit saith
unto the churches to him that overcometh will I give
to eat of the tree of life, which is in the midst of the
paradise of God.

"Lost In Myself"

The Lord gave me a talent and a heart to fulfill his

purpose. At times my pride makes it hard for my

Godly side to overshadow my wrong. People give me

compliments to lift me up but all I want to do is go

home. People want me to get lost in myself but I must

give Jesus the glory. He's the one that inspired me to

PROVERBS OF A TROUBLED SOUL

tell the world and about his virtue and tell the world

my story. Jesus is the only reason I'm making

it through my storms. The Lord knows I wouldn't

mind dying if helping the world wasn't the only

reason I was born. I often mask my misery with a

smile. The painful memories of my past tear at my

soul. How do I love my people of Detroit and they

curse the substance of my soul? Getting stoned is a

part of walking with Christ so I forgive you if you

smite me. A man has to take many stripes for the

chance at gaining life eternally. I'm all for the

priceless victory witnessing wonders and walking

down streets of Gold. I've seen hell in a dream before.

The son of perdition can keep his Gold. Glory be to

the Christ in the highest for paving the way to eternal

wealth. Even when you're down to zero dollars

having Christ is having help.

PROVERBS OF A TROUBLED SOUL

Proverbs 13:7

There is that maketh himself rich yet hath nothing
there is that maketh himself poor yet hath great
riches.

"There's A Time for Everything"

Many times I wonder why life is so strange. It seems

like nothing ever happens when you think it should. I

often wonder when will my time come because I feel

so ready that it should. Does feeling ready mean the

time is right? Many fighters thought they were ready

but when they stepped in the ring they loss the fight.

That leads me to understand that impatience

and overconfidence are foolish processes that conquer

the world. Even knowledge can lead us astray

because most of history remains untold. Chronology

has only existed for about 6,000 years so how can the

world's knowledge suffice for countless years of

PROVERBS OF A TROUBLED SOUL

unknown facts? 6,000 years of spotted history after the great book burning of Alexandria. It takes time to receive understanding you have run the race of life with stamina. With that being said true knowledge is reserved for the Lord above. If we knew what time the Lord was coming back would we be humble enough for the next level? I think a few people would be ready to fly. If the rapture was to come today I believe I would take my place in the sky. I knew it was time for change when I saw the skin of the damned and heard the voices of the demons from hell. The way of Christ is a gift that brings life it's our fault if we fail. It's a time to be lonely and it's a time to cry. It's a time to be happy and it's time to ask God why. It's time for us to love one another and stop putting each other down. When we do what Jesus wants us to do it takes time but it will turn around.

PROVERBS OF A TROUBLED SOUL
Ecclesiastes 3:4

A time to weep, and a time to laugh a time to mourn, and a time to dance.

"What I Came For"

Life seems to have more traps than safe havens. It's

like everything is vanity because living a life to

please to ourselves is being defiant to God. Becoming

your own God will result in misfortune because a

man's wisdom has limits. Planning to live in luxury is

a blessing until you honor extravagance more than the

doctrine of God. It seems like most people love to

praise Jesus when all is well but go astray when they

are tested with trouble. It would be grand if my name

was among the elite and I walked with giants every

day. I'm even guilty of questioning my calling when

things don't go my way. I'm ashamed of myself for

that because no prophet from the bible had it easy. I

just want Jesus to know that when I say I love him my

PROVERBS OF A TROUBLED SOUL

life proves to be pleasing. I just want what I came for but I'm beginning to have a change of heart. I also understand that I'm at a crossroad where everything seems apart. Many days I feel like my education has failed me because it has no power to comfort my troubled soul. I know the Prince of the Powers of Air does everything in his power to make me fold. The Lord gave me the spirit of a warrior and I will fight Satan until I crush his crown. Only with the help of Jesus can I defeat Beelzebub (Lord of The Flies) he's the strongest enemy around. I want what I came for but I'm going to follow God and do it right. I chose Jesus for the long-haul because I don't get caught up in the hype.

Luke 14:26

If any man come to me, and hate not his father, and mother, and wife, and children, and brethren, and

PROVERBS OF A TROUBLED SOUL
sisters, yea, and his own life also, he cannot be my
disciple.

"Insecurity"

Insecurity is a disease with no know remedy for

cure or vaccination. Insecurity ends marriages,

friendships, and sanity. Insecurity destroys kindness

and it sets back humanity. A chief principle of

happiness is the ability to accept the truth. A beautiful

woman will be coveted many suitors and handsome

male will have options as well. Insecurity is the father

of envy and the mother of delusion. If the

services BOTH PARTIES preform in a relationship

are sincere insecurity will not be a factor. A negative

mind will invite insecurity every time. A relationship

build on a foundation of truth will be not be infiltrated

by insecurity unless it is welcomed by fear or doubt.

One way to destroy this chief negative principle

PROVERBS OF A TROUBLED SOUL

called "Insecurity" is to be positive but not naive. A

person will be a slave to insecurity until he or she

break the chains of doubt. Insecurity will never

destroy my relationships because God protects my

heart and my brain. Beware of the power of insecurity

that demon will drive you insane.

Isaiah 26:3

Thou wilt keep him in perfect peace whose mind is
stayed on thee because he trusteth in thee.

"Worth Fighting For"

The closer we get to our dreams the more it feels like

they will never come to fruition. People will go out of

their way to downplay all your hopes as well as

your visions. You will ask yourself often are my

dreams worth fighting for and why was I born to

carry so many burdens? Everybody loves you when

you reach your fame but everybody will hate you

PROVERBS OF A TROUBLED SOUL

when you're hurting. Life is a complex test that most

people fail spiritual. Only a few people have the

courage to suffer and wait on the lord. In my life it

seems that nothing really makes sense but yet I refuse

to be bent. Lords knows I hate challenges but I hate

losing even more. I stand tall through it all there's no

surrender in this spiritual war. I believe in my heart a

righteous dream is worth fighting for. I often wonder

why my life is filled with so many unanswered

prayers and an abundance of needed friends. If quit

I'll be a loser and end up like the weakest of men. Our

dreams are worth fighting for so stand up and fight

until they come. The Lord is my shield and my

shepherd he'll never deny a good son.

Psalm 84:11

For the LORD God is a sun and shield the LORD will
give grace and glory no good thing will he withhold
from them that walk uprightly.

PROVERBS OF A TROUBLED SOUL
"I Wouldn't Pretend"

When I look in your eyes I am released from my

suffering. The stripes I endure for my transgressions

are nothing compare to the thought of you. How is it

that you captured me without intercourse? The bond

we have shall out last forever. I promise I shall be at

your side no matter the weather. I think of you when

I'm alone and I smile and then a single tear of

joy rolls down my face. They say never say never but

I could never forget the power of your embrace. The

Lord's angels hide their virtue in your smile. Your

elegance and intelligence demands my attention.

The passion I have for you no man in this world can

take. When we die don't worry our spirits shall meet

again. What I have for you is real I wouldn't dare

pretend.

Genesis 29:20

Jacob served seven years for Rachel and they seemed unto him but a few days for the love he had to her.

"Most Things Are Never Simple"

It feels like things should be so simple in life. Every

choice should be so black and white. I think this

would life make more amazing. I wish choices could

be as simple as if A then B if B then A in almost

every occasion. In reality the variables C, D, and F

always enter the equation. If a woman is beautiful,

faithful, god-fearing, well-mannered, and a great

lover her husband should love her. If a man is

handsome, earns a substantial salary, a gentleman,

god-fearing, and a great lover his wife should love

him. The problems that plague the world seem so

easy to solve. When a person has been poor for his or

her entire life when financial endowment comes that

PROVERBS OF A TROUBLED SOUL

person should be satisfied. If being rich is the answer

to life then why do some many rich people destroy

themselves with drugs or alcohol and whatever else?

Some rich men even commit suicide in hate of their

life. Why is it that every genius is an owner of a

troubled soul? These simple things in life have no

answer let the truth be told. Why does racism exist

and why is the world so cold? Why do people hate

one another for over material things? Why do we love

to put each other down and we're all meant to be

kings and queens? These questions exist because we

allow Satan to have his way. Why do some people

blame God for their trouble when they live for

themselves every day? I've came to the realization

that nobody understands life. If the life of rich men

is so perfect then why do even the wealthy know

PROVERBS OF A TROUBLED SOUL
strife? With wisdom comes pain only Godly

knowledge will win this fight.

Proverbs 3:5

Trust in the LORD with all thine heart and lean not
unto thine own understanding.

"A Pain That Won't Die"

Since you've been gone my heart refuses to heal. I

should be bitter knowing I won't see face again. You

were stolen from me by death sometimes I feel that

life can be so cruel. I'm so surprised that I have any

love left because it seems like love is for fools. When

I hear your name it feels time stands still. The

memory of your smile and charm puts me in a place

where I'm easy to harm. Who knows

heartbreak except someone that loved somebody and

lost them to a tragic fate? A million cries and a

million whys can't resurrect them from the

grave. This pain will always be burnt deep in my

heart. This is a situation that money can't change.

Many romances never manifest when we feel so

deserving and willing to make it official. This is a

pain that won't die the more I learn the more it

burns. I miss you more every day it's impossible to

express how I'm turned. To silence my mind's dark

places I put my misery in words. The only reason I

haven't gone insane is because I believe in God's

word.

Ecclesiastes 1:18

For in much wisdom is much grief: and he that
increaseth knowledge increaseth sorrow.

"The Prison of Our Mind"

My mind is a prison of memories that troubles me

when history repeats itself. The action of others has a

PROVERBS OF A TROUBLED SOUL

direct effect on our entire generation. When people repeat my life's errors he or she cannot understand the foolishness they resurrect. To lead people astray by imposing a mixed doctrine on the weak-minded is a tragedy that's acceptable for a corrupt purpose. The control of a person's mind gives you authority over that person's body as well. When we neglect knowledge and wisdom we welcome ignorance into our lives. The puzzles of life will not come to fruition unless you incorporate its pieces appropriately. The leadership of the blind as led many of our once strong brothers and sisters into a perpetual darkness. In this place of darkness demons feast on the souls of the Lost. Instead of worshipping God people worship entertainers and sometimes even their boss. Having an enlightened mind is a form freedom that cannot be purchased with money. It can only be bought when

PROVERBS OF A TROUBLED SOUL
you thirst for the truth. A man or woman equates to

nothing when their mind rejects actuality. Value true

wisdom over gold because critical thinking is the only

method that can simplify living. Don't fear isolation

because you speak the truth. Fear an abundance of

friends that idolize sinning.

Proverbs 3:13-20

Happy is the man that findeth wisdom, and the man
that getteth understanding. For the merchandise of it
is better than the merchandise of silver and the gain
thereof than fine gold. She is more precious than
rubies and all the things thou canst desire are not to
be compared unto her. Length of days is in her right
hand and in her left hand riches and honor. Her ways
are ways of pleasantness and all her paths are peace.
She is a tree of life to them that lay hold upon her:
and happy is every one that retaineth her. The Lord
by wisdom hath founded the earth by understanding
hath he established the heavens. By his knowledge the
depths are broken up and the clouds drop down the
dew.

PROVERBS OF A TROUBLED SOUL
"If You Love Me"

If you love me let me know so I can return to you

God's Greatest Gift. Jesus put us here love one

another and sometimes a person's spirit needs a lift.

Many people don't know anybody cares about their

troubles or their pain. If you love me inspire me when

I'm losing everything. If you love me despite

everything that's going wrong tell me I'm going to

be ok. If you love me give me the courage to endure

my afflictions and stand tall when I'm losing my way.

If you love me aspire to prove I can rise after I fall. If

you love me tell me don't be afraid when people say I

won't make it. If you love me don't let my heart

become sour when I feel like I can't take it. If you

love me encourage me to love people that hate me

when I only tried to help. If you love me when the

flame of my spirit is about to burn out give me the

PROVERBS OF A TROUBLED SOUL
love that I don't have for myself. If you love me

manifest the spiritual gifts that I need but can't seem

to afford. It's so easy to quit when things get hard and

it seems that doing good has no real reward. The

power of a kind word is underrated but it's

virtue heals the wounds of the soul. I love all my

friends and if we keep the faith we won't be left in the

cold.

Matthew 22:36-40

Master which is the great commandment in the law?
Jesus said unto him thou shalt love the Lord thy God
with all thy heart, and with all thy soul, and with all
thy mind. This is the first and great commandment.
And the second is like unto it Thou shalt love thy
neighbor as thyself. On these two commandments
hang all the law and the prophets.

"True Love In A Special Way"

When I was at my lowest you took time to hear my

sorrow. You always give me the impression that if

PROVERBS OF A TROUBLED SOUL

could make it through the dark times I will see light

tomorrow. When I was brokenhearted you gave me

the will to stay strong. Every time I felt quitting you

made me feel like holding on. Through all the

tribulations you keep me from losing my mind. Some

people just want to be rich or bask in fame but our

relationship puts Gold to shame. That's why every

Sunday I report to church to thank you for your grace.

Your love is tough and sometimes you allow the

enemy too utterly beat me down. Then you give me

courage to dust it off and get up for another round.

Father you have given me wisdom in abundance.

Much of this wisdom I'm too young to have the

Privilege to understand. As my prestige grows I

witness your glory and it continues to be grand.

Thank you Jesus for showing me true Love in a

PROVERBS OF A TROUBLED SOUL
special way. I love you father and I can't wait to see

on your return day.

Psalm 34: 1-6

I will bless the Lord at all times his praise shall
continually be in my mouth. My soul shall make her
boast in the Lord the humble shall hear thereof and be
glad. O magnify the Lord with me and let us exalt his
name together. I sought the Lord, and he heard me
and delivered me from all my fears. They looked unto
him and were lightened and their faces were not
ashamed. This poor man cried and the Lord heard him
and saved him out of all his troubles.

"It Starts With Me First"

When people ask me for advice sometimes it's a

challenge to find the words to say. Who I am to tell

somebody they can't change. I'm living proof that

change happens every day. I understand that all

change starts first with one's self. A man that only

honors himself is too immature to receive greatness it

takes sacrifice. I just want to do the right things

PROVERBS OF A TROUBLED SOUL
because I never felt good about doing wrong. The

fruits of fidelity feed the soul and leads it to a

righteous destination. A true friend will listen to

reason and sometimes failure is a blessing. I have

freewill to do as I wish I'm responsible for my own

progression.

Matthew 7: 4-5

Or how wilt thou say to thy brother, Let me pull out
the mote out of thine eye; and, behold, a beam is in
thine own eye? Thou hypocrite, first cast out the
beam out of thine own eye; and then shalt thou see
clearly to cast out the mote out of thy brother's eye.

"I Don't Know Everything"

If a man is eager for war in his mind he has nothing to

live for. A lifetime of disappointment will corrupt the

heart of the weak-spirited man. Who knows pain

except one who has endured its trials? The loss of

love can poison a man's mind forever and the cruel

PROVERBS OF A TROUBLED SOUL

venom of separation shall bring tears to the mightiest

of men. Life is no fairy tale every life will not have a

happy end. Marriages sometimes end because they

were manifested on the wrong grounds. Love based

solely on financial status will surely be bitter and the

bells of shame shall sound. A person who is blessed

with the gift of wisdom must be willing to teach and

preach. A good leader loves his followers and he

teaches them virtuous things. A good man loves a

virtuous wife because her values are those of a queen.

Love wisdom more than ornaments and give your

heart to your dreams. I don't know everything but

from my wisdom I shall be a King.

Proverbs 4:5-6

Get wisdom, get understanding forget it not neither
decline from the words of my mouth. Forsake her not,
and she shall preserve thee love her, and she shall
keep thee.

PROVERBS OF A TROUBLED SOUL
"Wearing A Mask"

My world is torn in fragments I mask my pain with a

smile. I've been feeling like this for much longer than

a little while. On the days that I think of you I wish I

could travel back in time. My heart is full of

sorrowful songs that nobody cares to hear. I really

believed in my heart you were the one that was

supposed to be my wife. Though you showed me

signs that you didn't feel same I loved you

nevertheless. It's not a day that goes pass that I don't

think about you as least twice. Since you've been

deceased I've wore a smile to disguise my pain. I

cover my heart with a shield I could never love a

woman the same. The pain that Jesus suffered is the

only thing greater than my depression since you've

been gone. I long for death in the late hours of the

PROVERBS OF A TROUBLED SOUL

night when I feel like I can't go on. The only thing

that keeps me going is the assignment the Lord gave

to me. If it wasn't for Jesus I know for a fact your

death would have drove me crazy. All

the achievements I acquire on this earth mean nothing

to me because you're not here to see me shine. I lost

you and I lost my father and God still managed to

keep my mind. I know you want me to go and strive

hard for a promising future. Jasmine I hope you

understand that without you or my father it feels like

there is no future. I can't wait until the Lord sends me

home to take my place in glory. Sometimes I hate that

I ever existed and I curse my birth. I just want to feel

loved instead of hated while I'm at home. Lord Jesus I

ask you to continue to hold me together I know it

won't be long. When I reach my final destination I'm

going to be set with riches untold. Thank you Jesus

for hearing my prayers and keeping me from losing

my soul.

2 Corinthians 4:16

For which cause we faint not but though our outward man perish yet the inward man is renewed day by day.

"The World"

The world wants to silence me because I understand

the tricks of the beast. Everything is going has

planned by the "Prince of Darkness" except me

holding my peace. Satan has offered me women and a

fast way out of a life with financial struggles. When I

served sin I didn't know myself I was willing to do

almost anything to anybody to increase in material

wealth. I made my blood offering at the age 19 and

since that day I've seen many things I shouldn't have

seen. Jesus allowed me to see the truth even when I

PROVERBS OF A TROUBLED SOUL

was blind to his majesty. I defied Christ to his face

and yet he had mercy on my blasphemy. Many days

I hoped for more and when I had more it still wasn't

enough. I created a problem I couldn't manage and

only Jesus could fix it up. I once walked with Satan in

vain because I hated the tests and trials that prove an

individual's worth. I know now that the favor of Jesus

is better than anything on earth. The power of money

is limited but Jesus's power comes from an endless

supply. Riches on earth makes life a lot easier and

most people don't have the patience to wait on the

Lord. Satan uses our impatience against us and offers

mankind a vain reward. Satan doesn't tell you about

all the foul things that shall transpire for you choosing

him as your Lord. You will lose the people closest to

you even when you renounce the ways of hell. I'm

still paying a price for once choosing evil but

PROVERBS OF A TROUBLED SOUL

remember good shall always prevail. The plan of

Satan is not structured for him to win he's in a lose-

lose situation. Satan and his followers shall surely pay

the ultimate price in the end. Jehovah judges all

things and no darkness can escape his light. Now that

I know Jesus the world the hates me more every day.

I can live with that though carrying a cross is the

price I have to pay.

Matthew 4: 3-10

And when the tempter came to him he said if thou be
the Son of God, command that these stones be made
bread. But he answered and said it is written man
shall not live by bread alone but by every word that
proceedeth out of the mouth of God. Then the devil
taketh him up into the holy city and setteth him on a
pinnacle of the temple. And saith unto him if thou be
the Son of God cast thyself down for it is written he
shall give his angels charge concerning thee and in
their hands they shall bear thee up lest at any time
thou dash thy foot against a stone. Jesus said unto him
it is written again thou shalt not tempt the Lord thy
God. Again the devil taketh him up into an exceeding
high mountain and sheweth him all the kingdoms of
the world and the glory of them and saith unto him all

these things will I give thee if thou wilt fall down and worship me. Then saith Jesus unto him get thee hence Satan for it is written thou shalt worship the Lord thy God and him only shalt thou serve.

"Sometimes Less Is More"

I tried to gain your interest to no avail I'm bitter

because I tried hard and still managed to fail. I

thought that if I showed you love that was never

shown to me I would surely prevail. I must admit I'll

miss hearing your beautiful voice and seeing

your angelic face. I've failed at love but I don't know

what I'm doing wrong. I've learned sometimes when

you want things to go right it's usually the same song.

I can only be me and that's all I can do. If being you

isn't enough for somebody that person isn't for you.

Sometimes less is more because a quick end can

prevent a disastrous situation. Don't change who you

PROVERBS OF A TROUBLED SOUL
are for love most of the time we just have to be

patient.

Jeremiah 2:33
Why trimmest thou thy way to seek love? therefore
hast thou also taught the wicked ones thy ways.

"Stand and Fight"

I still shine through the drama no matter how many

storms come I refuse to fold. I've been told I would

never I amount nothing. I've been stood up on many

dates. I've been told I would always be a fat slob but

that negative feedback inspired me to fight hard.

Sometimes I feel like I could cry all night but then my

spirit tells me to stand and fight. I almost lost my life

in a few battles and I have scars and wisdom to show

for it. That's why I know the earth is a spiritual place

contrary to what people think. The way the world is

PROVERBS OF A TROUBLED SOUL

set up it discourages you from believing in anything

spiritual. I faced my fears and came out victorious.

Overcoming a situation that should have killed you is

always glorious. The deceptions that confuse us every

day makes it hard to tell what a righteous path is. I

count on faith to get by standing and fighting because

heaven is where my heart is.

1 Timothy 6:12
Fight the good fight of faith, lay hold on eternal life,
whereunto thou art also called, and hast professed a
good profession before many witnesses.

"When It's All Gone"

Lord Jesus I will trust you when it's all gone and I

have nothing to call my own. Lord I know I will

recover what Satan stole. I stand with you Jesus until

you bring me home. When it's all gone I know you

can make me whole again. The stripes I've endured

PROVERBS OF A TROUBLED SOUL

waiting on the day you'll save me have been great

indeed. In this season in my life I've seen things I

wish I wouldn't have seen. Lord Jesus I call on your

name in unusual pain because I have nowhere else to

turn. My friends talk behind my back and call me a

fool for trusting in you. Lord why does life have to be

so unfair I feel like I'm living in hell. Why does it

seem like everyone with power over me loves to see

me lose? Some days I feel buried alive and my

fighting spirit is made weary and inadequate. When

it's all gone why do people kick and spit on their

fellow man? I must admit I sometimes feel ashamed

because I chose to walk with you. I had to sacrifice

petty things for eternal substance. Jesus when I call

your name for help it feels like you're not listening

but nevertheless I call. Death must be sweet

compared to the prison of my life I'm so tired it all. I

PROVERBS OF A TROUBLED SOUL

accept this punishment for my sins. Please forgive me

Lord for all the hurt I caused. I don't deserve your

grace I deserve to be resting in the dirt or living in a

dark place. Though it's all gone and nothing is left I

will trust you through it all. Lord you gave me the

strength to live by faith instead of busting my fist

against a wall.

Isaiah 40:31

But they that wait upon the Lord shall renew their
strength; they shall mount up with wings as eagles;
they shall run, and not be weary; and they shall walk,
and not faint.

"Waiting On My Time"

Through all my drama I understand that some people

need a shoulder to cry on. I never had that shoulder

and plus I didn't want to be a burden. I question

myself and God on the daily basis. I ask God is love

really unconditional? I ask God why do you send me

PROVERBS OF A TROUBLED SOUL

to comfort people and no comforter is sent to me in

my time of pain? The world seems so backward to me

it almost feels like some type of game. Most of my

brothers and sisters would rather have material

success rather than prosper in the Holy Spirit. The

doctrines of the world's leaders have transformed to

earth a low paradise. Who created these rules that evil

men made suffice? The world's laws pervert God's

law and the perpetrators are exalted to fame and

glory. Where is the justice in this world filled with

filth and crime? In these modern times marriage is

joke and so is everything that was

once deemed divine. These trying times have

transformed my heart into stone and I don't know if

I want it to be flesh again. I find it hard befriending

anybody the world is against me until my very end.

My own older brother has been my enemy since birth.

PROVERBS OF A TROUBLED SOUL

I feel so alone in this world but yet I'm still able to

smile. I thank God for that small miracle because

that's all I had for a while. I'm just waiting on my

time writing my tears into words as I keep a positive

mind.

2 Timothy 2:3
Thou therefore endure hardness as a good soldier of
Jesus Christ

"Why Let The Devil Win"

If you commit a small crime that same crime you can

send to jail. If you commit a small sin that same small

sin can condemn you to hell. Since we know the right

path to follow why do some people choose to fail? In

life I believe that mental suffering is only a few steps

above perdition. Physical wounds heal quickly but

what can soothe the fall out of shame? Though God

didn't promise us a perfect life on earth he did

PROVERBS OF A TROUBLED SOUL

promise he would make things better. Sin is a reality

that can never be justified but it can be forgiven

through change. Don't let a painful past block your

gift of eternal living. Heaven is a realm of joy where

things that never age and never fade. I believe in a

better life so I'm an advocate for a greater age. A

person cannot defeat Satan if their heart is filled with

foolish practices that appall God. The way of the

world will not stand because of the wickedness that

lies within. Be still and wait on the Lord why should

you let the devil win?

Matthew 16: 26-27

For what is a man profited if he shall gain the whole
world and lose his own soul? Or what shall a man
give in exchange for his soul? For the Son of man
shall come in the glory of his Father with his angels
and then he shall reward every man according to his
works.

PROVERBS OF A TROUBLED SOUL
"American Idols"

We allowed ourselves to make people of renowned Gods because our brethren bow down to them in worship. We follow the beliefs of celebrities and endear them more than we take heed to the doctrine of God. How do we shape our lives after people we don't know and they don't care to know us? I can see this is a part of the devil's plan. He exalts evil men to high places because most people will follow the ways of rich men. Abundance of money is synonymous with being Holy in the eyes of the world. Nobody wants to carry a cross but it's something the Lord's people have to do. I hope America wakes up from its slumber because God this country is far from you. People would rather believe in fables than follow in God's path to life. American Idols are false Gods it's only wise to praise Jesus.

PROVERBS OF A TROUBLED SOUL

2 Timothy 4:4

And they shall turn away their ears from the truth and shall be turned unto fables.

"It's Possible"

Life can take us places we don't want to go but

unpleasant situations make a person strong. Time and

time again our dreams seem so farfetched but they are

possible if we dare to hold on. Most of the time

dreams materialize in our darkest hour. We need to

understand that living by faith is the only power.

When miracles manifest they give no warning

because the Lord loves to surprise. You're not a fool

for believing in your dreams when we give up Satan

has his prize. It's possible to be better than mediocre

greatness comes after tests and trials. Mediocrity is

bliss when excellence seems unattainable. Let the

naysayers live a life that they hate. As believers we

PROVERBS OF A TROUBLED SOUL

must the keep hope alive. It's possible to accomplish

things of substance even when experts forecast our

demise. We can make a positive impact on the earth

when we let the word of God prevail. A coward will

give up on their dreams a true champion never quits.

Knowing our dreams are possible is knowledge of

God's word. It's possible to accomplish our dreams

even in the face of defeat. When we have God we

always have a chance to compete. I'm just stating the

facts Christ brought me though when I was weak.

Hebrews 12: 1-3

Therefore we also since we are surrounded by so
great a cloud of witnesses let us lay aside every
weight and the sin which so easily ensnares us and let
us run with endurance the race that is set before
us looking unto Jesus the author and finisher of our
faith who for the joy that was set before Him endured
the cross, despising the shame, and has sat down at
the right hand of the throne of God. For consider him
who endured such hostility from sinners against
himself lest you become weary and discouraged in
your souls.

PROVERBS OF A TROUBLED SOUL

"So Much Time Has Passed"

Lord so much time has passed since I've known

happiness. When I'm alone I can't help but wonder do

you really care if I have joy. The promises

from the bible haven't materialized as I imagined. In

my spare time all I think about is woe is me. My

complaining is no different from the Hebrews as they

traveled through the wilderness. You've brought me

so far but it seems like I have so far to go. Why do I

feel like I'm losing my grace in the time I need it the

most? Why do people that I thought were my friends

slander my name in secret? Lord this storm you set

before me is shaking my faith and my body is stricken

with pain. Lord you really want me to forgive the

very people who curse my name. This walk is more

difficult that than I ever could imagine. So much time

has passed since I counted my blessings. All the great

PROVERBS OF A TROUBLED SOUL

things you've done for me yet I seem to forget. My

impatience is clouding my judgment and

my frustration is leading me to hate the path of

truth. Lord I just need you strengthen me again

because this is the only fight a person needs to win.

Following Jesus is never easy and to do it correctly I

must sacrifice all things sparing nothing. So much

time has passed since I've done what I wanted to do.

For a chance at living forever this is what I have to

do.

Matthew 10:22

And ye shall be hated of all men for my name's sake
but he that endureth to the end shall be saved.

"Walking Toward The Unknown"

Sometimes I feel like I must be crazy for having faith.

To truly have faith one must walk blindly toward the

unknown. Who knows what's waiting for me

PROVERBS OF A TROUBLED SOUL

tomorrow and I question is living worth my time. The

unknown can be very exciting but it also can steal

your mind. What do you do when you don't have the

motivation to go on? What do you do when it seems

like the only way out of misery is living a life that's

all wrong? I often feel as if the lord has forgotten me

in this unknown place of darkness and

disappointment. In this walk toward the unknown a

person will be antagonized. I usually feel like it

would be much easier to die rather than living on.

This walk of faith toward the unknown is one I wish I

could avoid there's been so much anguish along the

way. How do I keep a positive mind when following

my dreams hasn't paid? Therefore walking toward the

unknown can only be done by the brave. This walk is

often a lonely walk but believe you can make it to the

next stage. Don't concentrate on your trials focus on

PROVERBS OF A TROUBLED SOUL

the future old things pass away. Walking toward the

unknown is not glamorous but it pays a dividend

that's mightier than any man can pay. Walking

toward the unknown shows you how to be still when

people count you out. Pray to draw strength from the

Lord until Jesus pays out.

2 Corinthians 10: 4-5

For the weapons of our warfare are not carnal, but
mighty through God to the pulling down of strong
holds. Casting down imaginations, and every high
thing that exalteth itself against the knowledge of
God, and bringing into captivity every thought to the
obedience of Christ.

"A Person's Path"

The path a person's chooses is always spiritual.

The actions of a man manifest from the purest portion

of a person's heart. This is true because where the

passion of a person resides the heart is not far from it.

Did not the boldness of Jesus's sacrifice provide a

PROVERBS OF A TROUBLED SOUL

second chance to all mankind? Did not the path of the

Holy Spirit give Christ and his apostles the power to

raise the dead from the grave as well as give sight to

the blind? On this path to righteousness I've learned

that nothing can withstand the power of love. Even

when I'm hard from head to toe it feels great to know

my help comes from above. A person's path will

bring you challenges that God will watch hoping that

you will choose him and succeed. A person's path in

life should not be about indulging in the flesh and

things of greed. A person's path should be about

nurturing people with hope and planting Godly seeds.

The path we choose proves who we are in our hearts.

If you turn out to be evil when you reach your success

you were always evil from the start.

Matthew 15: 18
But those things which proceed out of the mouth
come forth from the heart and they defile the man.

PROVERBS OF A TROUBLED SOUL
"Don't Please Men Please God"

Most people will never appreciate how much love
that you show. Even when you say yes to their
requests when you should said no. What are the
chances of pleasing somebody who hated you from
the start? Sometimes the person you lay with does not
have your best interest at heart. Some men and
women are envious of their own partners because
they share a perverted love. Life is so hard sometimes
a person will doubt Jesus's love. Just know that some
people will hate you for whatever you do. Aim to
please God and not men because Christ really loves
you.

Proverbs 29:2
The fear of man lays a snare but whoever trusts in the
Lord is safe.

PROVERBS OF A TROUBLED SOUL
"No Smiles In The Wilderness"

It's easy to smile when your future looks bright and
you seem to get blessed every time you turn around.
When you have that special somebody in your life it's
so logical to praise God. I wonder why when
circumstances change for the worse it's so easy to
forget God. Some people live a life of luxury for
years and when their prosperity ends so does their
relationship with the Lord. OOO how easy is it to
smile when you can do no wrong? How easy is it to
curse God when your life is a sad song? It's hard to
smile in the wilderness because hope seems so far
away. When you're in the wilderness it's a challenge
to find a happy place for a moment in a day. We must
remember the wilderness is God's test of our Love.
Testing a person with tribulation is how we are
perfected in Christ's blood. There's no smiles in the

PROVERBS OF A TROUBLED SOUL

wilderness but remember there's always hope. Never

let trying times darken your heart because your faith

will break your yoke.

Hebrews 3: 7-8

Wherefore as the Holy Ghost saith, today if ye will
hear his voice, harden not hearts, as in the
provocation, in the day of temptation in the
wilderness.

"What Does It All Mean"

Sometimes I wonder what it all means. I wonder if I

would really be happy if I had everything. Does a

man have the authority to put a price on his soul?

When I watch the news everything seems so bleak

and the world looks so cold. If I belonged to an elite

social class would I forget the torturous struggle that

made me consider suicide? What I wouldn't give to

live in a world where nobody lied. What does it mean

to be in a world that's not familiar with truth? Why do

PROVERBS OF A TROUBLED SOUL

college degrees have no value without the right

people blessing you? When I became a man I fully

understood that the world is full of deceptions. The

only one who has the answer to life is God I had to

learn that lesson. I searched for answers to life in

other places and I found nothing but half-truths. Why

is it that when your heart wants to live righteously

God allows Satan to make our lives so hard? Does

anybody understand the concept of riches untold? The

pressure of affliction shall refine our souls as precious

gems. We only get one time to pass the test of life and

who knows when the test ends. I don't know what it

all means but I know I'm going to fight until I win. I

wonder why taking a step toward the unknown and

mysterious is so hard to do? I don't know what it all

means but Jesus I trust in you.

Job 23: 10

PROVERBS OF A TROUBLED SOUL
But he that knoweth the way that I take: when he hath
tried me I shall come forth as gold.

"I Stayed"

I stayed when it was so easy to walk away. I went

against my intellect and worldly knowledge to carry a

cross and pray. I stayed when everybody I knew

couldn't help me or let me down. These were same

people I broke my back for and they treated me like a

clown. I stayed when in my heart I so badly I wanted

to quit. I prayed for my life to prosper when failure

was all I could get. I stayed when the woman I loved

was killed and my soul was scarred to the core. I

stayed when I had to donate plasma just to keep gas

in my car. The two years I donated plasma I learned

the hearts of men. Many people enter your life to put

you down I wish this was pretend. I stayed when my

father died and I wanted to join him in death. I stayed

when things got a little better and I could finally catch

my breath. I stayed because I have faith and I live my

life for you. I stayed because you're Jesus and I

choose to suffer like you.

1 Peter 2:21
For even hereunto were ye called: because Christ also
suffered for us, leaving us an example, so that ye
should follow his footstep.

"Uncharted Territory"

As I travel down the road of life I realize the world is

ever changing. How blessed is the soul that survives

a struggle? What man can tell you the results of

tomorrow? It's best to live life with a smile it's

pointless to drown yourself in shame. I think of every

day as an opportunity no yesterday is the same as the

future. I enjoy the surprises of life that uncharted

PROVERBS OF A TROUBLED SOUL

territory is certain to provide. Though some surprises

are unwanted there's a reason for each challenge that

we can't comprehend. The idea of uncharted territory

gives me hope and it also allows me to dream. I

question would life be worth living if I really knew

everything? It's hard to imagine living life day by day

without a chance of seeing something new. It's fun to

be able to say "I don't know how I did it

but nevertheless I made it though." Uncharted

territory intrigues my soul and leads me to pursue

my goals zealously. I keep my head to the

zenith no matter what because I know the Lord is

testing me.

Hebrews 11:1

Now faith is the substance for thing hoped for, the

evidence of things not seen.

PROVERBS OF A TROUBLED SOUL
"The Friend Zone"

The friend zone is dreaded but it is often a blessing in disguise. Intimate interest usually blinds us from the truth. The friend zone keeps us from nurturing emotions that we don't need. The friend zone teaches us about the character of someone in whom we have interest. How can we love somebody as a wife or a husband without loving them first as a friend? The friend zone teaches us the virtue and substance of being patient. Only a fool rushes to be with somebody they don't fully understand. Failure is a product of impatience more times than not. A person's beauty is deceitful it can hide the corruption of a bad crop. People change on their own time don't live life like it's a race. If you skip the friend zone you're only putting yourself in a bad space.

PROVERBS OF A TROUBLED SOUL

1 Kings 11: 4

For it came to pass, when Solomon was old that his wives turned his heart away after their gods: and his heart was not perfect with the lord God his God, as was the heart of his father David.

"My Father My Friend"

I always wanted to match your light because almost everybody who met you loved you on sight. You were more than a father you were my friend. We always kept it honest with each other because we don't know how to pretend. Everything that I am I owe to you. Your genes gave me what it takes to do what I do. I have no sadness I only have joy. I wear your name like a badge of honor I'm proud to be your boy. I promise to look after my mother and my family like I promised to do. You're my father and my closest friend I was blessed to have you.

PROVERBS OF A TROUBLED SOUL
Exodus 20:12
Honour thy father and thy mother: that thy days may
be long upon the land which the lord thy thy God
Giveth thee.

"The Giving Spirit"

The desperate face of the homeless is dreaded on

streets by people who can easily help. Nobody cares

about a homeless person's story. Only a few

people have mercy on others with nowhere to

go. When I can I take time to be kind because in the

future who knows where their life will go.

To give what is earned through hard work comes only

from a heart that is inspired by God. Lord knows it's

not simple to give and nobody cared if you had

it hard. Everybody remembers when their personal

storm came. The times when our own families

laughed in secret as we suddenly lost everything.

PROVERBS OF A TROUBLED SOUL

Even when our painful memories steal our joy we

cannot let our giving spirit die. Think of the substance

we waste foolishly. Think of every time we wasted

money on things we don't need. The same money we

wasted doing nothing we denied the

homeless because of our greed. The giving spirit is a

spirit of love it is designed to take us far. You may

not be famous in the opinion of the world but to those

you help Jesus makes you a star.

Proverbs 19:17

He that hath pity upon the poor lendeth unto the Lord;
that which he hath given will he pay him again.

"My Anger"

My anger knows no bounds so please stay out of my

way. I only wanted to be peaceful but only trouble

comes my way. Why do people choose to push my

buttons when I feel so ready to snap? Why do I feel

PROVERBS OF A TROUBLED SOUL
like God left me alone to survive inside a trap? Only

my prayers have the power to keep my rage in

control. It's hard to use temperance when you're ready

when folly in your soul. I know better than letting my

anger transform me into a beast. Anger will destroy

us all so knowing this it must cease.

Proverbs 27:3
A stone is heavy, and the sand weighty; but a fool's
wrath is heavier than them both.

"I'm Tired"

I'm tired of expecting better and getting worse!!! I'm

tired of feeling like my life is a curse!!! I'm tired of

being patient I want what I have coming now. I'm

tired of pretending to be happy when my whole world

is crashing down. I'm tired of being thankful for

things that were less than what I wanted. I'm tired of

taking chances on people when my heart can't afford

it. I'm tired of dealing with people I can't stand that

makes me sick to my stomach. I'm tired of memories

that block my excitement when I accomplish

something great. I'm tired of the women I meet

turning out to be snakes. I'm tired of my kindness

being taken for weakness. I'm so tired of the word

"wait." I'm tired of my life because it never goes how

I want it to go. I'm tired of being tired I've never been

this tired before!!!

Galatians 6:9
And let us not be weary in well-doing for in due
season we shall reap if we faint not.

"Leave It In God's Hands"

When you've lost the only reason you had to live it's

simple for us to question God's plan. It's also easy to

become bitter and follow the doctrine of the broken

PROVERBS OF A TROUBLED SOUL

man. The trials that God allows into our lives are

meant to build character but it seems like we

won't survive. To be honest I still can't explain the

hurt I felt when I found out my father died. My father

was my joy and my hate I only wanted to make him

proud. I always will miss the days when we

would joke and we both would laugh out loud. I'm

leaving my sorrow in God's hands because my father

wants to see me win. When God takes who you love

the most trust and believe a miracle is in the wind.

Trust in the lord with your whole heart and never let

doubt change your mind. Be of good courage and

stand tall with Jesus believe we will survive.

Psalms 27:14

Wait on the lord be of good courage and he shall
strengthen thine heart wait I say on the Lord.

PROVERBS OF A TROUBLED SOUL
"Why"

Why do the most powerful lessons have to be learned

through suffering? Why do some people hate when

others make it out of a tight situation? Why does the

whole world urge you to move in a rush when

God tells us be patient? Why is foolish behavior

honored more than the ways of the wise? Why do

some people wish the worse on you and then smile as

you're passing by? Why are children educated by

history teachers that reciprocate falsehoods? Why do

some people pretend to be righteous but their

hearts hold vanity? Why do some people live to

spread confusion gossiping about other people until it

brings about their own ruin? Why does love just seem

like it's merely a word? Why do some people hate the

uncomfortable truth but love living in a comfortable

fraud? Why do I love people that hate me? Why do I

PROVERBS OF A TROUBLED SOUL
hate telling lies when the truth makes people forsake

me? Asking why leads to nowhere so do what's right

in your heart. All the answers are coming soon until

then humble your heart.

James 3: 17
But the wisdom that is from above is first pure, then
peaceable, gentle, and easy to be intreated, full of
mercy and good fruits, without partiality, and without
hypocrisy.

"Money"

Money brings out who you really rather it be good or

bad. Money makes everything better and it makes

everything worse. Money ends marriages and it keeps

marriages together. Is money evil for relieving the

truth that kind of makes me wonder? Money didn't

force people to live life by the sword. People choose

the road to perdition for quick reward. Greed is really

to blame for most of the chaos that affects earth. A

PROVERBS OF A TROUBLED SOUL

man's soul is never satisfied not many people aren't

content with enough. I want that Benz but I don't

want to earn it the right way. I want a stable of

beautiful women I can have sex with in the same day.

People are misguided by foolish men who got caught

up in the hype. When money is flowing well the

intoxication of sin makes it seem right. Some people

live their whole life chasing a lie. Who goes against

the laws of the Lord and he or she shall not surely

die? Look at them now they were bold enough to go

against God's rules. Now they're begging Jesus to

release them from a sweltering fiery tomb. The fires

of hell burn their flesh and smell is so toxic they can't

breathe. Follow the rules of Jesus Christ or end up

where they didn't believe.

Proverbs 11: 28

He that trusteth in his riches shall fall; but the
righteous shall flourish as a branch.

"Yes We Can Yes We did"

One of Satan's greatest tricks is self-doubt because if you don't believe in yourself how can you believe in God? I'm sure many of us have been told by dream-killers that we would never amount to nothing. That negativity the haters gave us made us try until we became something. I was told I wouldn't live to see 21 and I'm happy to say I look 21 at 29. I was told I would never live to do something positive but I didn't listen to the Devil and his lies. People will attack you with your past when they see you have a future. All that discouraging feedback did was motivate us until we did something super. We stood in the longest lines imaginable to get our piece of the pie. Some people took the easy route but now they hate themselves and they wonder why. I remember when some people laughed when I went back to school. I have my

Bachelor's degree working on my Master's degree

now who's the fool? It's more to life than doing the

same things you did as a kid. Just look at how far we

came from where we started. Yes we can and yes we

did!!!

Proverbs 23: 7
For as he thinketh in heart in his heart, so is he: eat
and drink, he saith to thee; but his heart is not with
thee.

"Old Wounds"

How do we get over the old wounds that seem to

mold our future? I'm talking about the

spiritual scars that last for generations. I've learned

that to truly overcome old wounds a person must

become familiar with pain. The trials of life turn out

to be jewels of knowledge forged through the process

of shame. How can I say goodbye to yesterday when

it felt better than my present-day? I was once told that

sunshine comes after the rain. I'm just waiting to be

healed of my old wounds by the word of the Prince of

Peace. Time reveals all answers and bears medicine

that cure the soul. It will always be a mystery why

people struggle so hard with these scars of old. All I

know is to keep praying because somehow I'm

making it through the storm. When all else fails trust

in the Bible it keeps me warm.

Job 13:15

Though he slay me, yet will I trust in him: but I will
maintain mine own ways before him.

"Is This My Ending"

Every morning I wake up with a sadness over things I

can't change. Am I asking for too much by asking

PROVERBS OF A TROUBLED SOUL

God for peace of mind? Sometimes I feel like I'm

going insane. Why is the remembrance of misery the

best education a person can have? Why is suffering

the true mother of humility? Why is diligence the true

father of glory? I believe happiness exists but it just

takes time to manifest. I know I will be fine one day

but in my mind it's like I'm dying every day. The

Lord tells me my son be strong you can make it don't

forget I'm on the throne. How many times did I

emerge from the dirt? I'll never quit until I finish

God's work. I know God has goal for me to reach.

Without my misery how could I really preach? I

know the Lord has a plan I can't see. It's not the end

I'm the child of victory.

Job 2:9-10

Then his wife said unto to him, doest thou still retain
thine integrity? Curse God, and die. But he said thou
speakest as one of the foolish women speaketh. What
shall we receive good at the hand of God and shall we

PROVERBS OF A TROUBLED SOUL
not receive evil? In all this did not Job sin with his
lips.

"I Don't Have A Reason"

Everything I've trusted in has failed me I don't have a

reason to feel joy. I wonder if I'm being overly

pessimistic or has life just beaten me down to the

bone? I don't have a reason to love anybody

because all my life I've been alone. How many life

cycles does it take to heal a broken heart? Who knows

what the future holds? Will I ever make it out of the

dark? My logic doesn't console my spirit so how far

does my education really take me? Finding value in

life is impossible without having reason to go on.

Everyone around you can praise your every move but

if you don't feel the positive energy life feels wrong.

Despite not having any visible motivation something

PROVERBS OF A TROUBLED SOUL

keeps telling me to live on. I've had enough of feeling

like I don't have a reason to live. If that was true by

now I would be long gone. Finding your purpose

takes longer than day and patience is the key to

making it home. I do have a reason to live and it's to

help people like me stay strong.

Jeremiah 29:11

For I know the thoughts I think toward you, saith the
Lord. Thoughts of peace and not evil to give you and
expected end.

"When You're Going A Through Struggle"

When you're going through a struggle nobody cares

about what you think or how you feel. When you're

going through a struggle most women show you

minimal respect. When you're going through a

struggle people are so quick to tell you the truth and

PROVERBS OF A TROUBLED SOUL
kick you while you're down. When you're going

through a struggle you wonder if blessings still exist

and if so why don't they come down. When

you're going through a struggle you have to work

twice as hard in anything you do. When you're going

through a struggle you have to have a special

personality for people to deal with you. When

you're going through a struggle nobody cares if you

die. When you are going through a struggle people

take you for a joke. When you're going through a

struggle people say "I hate you I hope you die broke."

When you're going through a struggle people question

is love real. When you're going through a struggle

you become a victim to people who have more skills.

Knowing all these facts I ask myself where is the

love. Is this the example of life that Jesus set when

murders spilled his blood?

```

## Proverbs 19: 17

All the brethren of the poor do hate him: how much more do his friends go far from him? He pursueth them with words, yet they are wanting to him.

# "Logic Can Be Your Worst Enemy"

Nobody knows what the future holds but the heavenly father. Our logic often slows down the process of breakthroughs. The problem with us educated people is we make things seem impossible when Jesus can do all things. Satan appoints so many people into our lives to make it seem as if he has the most excellent authority. It's still a mystery to me why Adam and Eve made life so hard. It's so easy to believe that the God's path will not prevail because it's such a hard path to walk. To be effective in the body of Christ we can't let logic poison our spiritual thoughts. The things of spirit are just that we must use our celestial
```

PROVERBS OF A TROUBLED SOUL
minds. Worldly logic only brings despair and

misfortune so therefore it's an enemy of mine.

1 Corinthians 2:14
But the natural man receiveth not the things of spirit
of God, for they are foolishness unto him; neither can
they know them, because they are spiritually
discerned.

"Who Am I"

I'm disappointed often but who am I to be treated

fair? Maybe I deserve all of the stripes and the

unfortunate reality in which I do exist. Who Am I to

be happy when I caused some much misery and led

people astray? I cover my pain with a smile who am I

to possess joy anyway? When was the last time I

was happy about my achievements I honestly don't

remember. I feel like my life is a cruel joke that God

laughs at daily. Who am I to love somebody when

nobody ever really loved me? I've been stood up, lied

on, and mistreated who am I to think love is for me?

Who am I to be kind when being selfish takes me so

far? It's my responsibility to love regardless of what

other people do. I am a son of the most high so who

am I not to love you?

Mark 13:13

And ye shall be hated of all men for my name's sake:
but he that shall endure unto the end, the same shall
be saved.

"Control"

Control is something most people want but none are

able to attain. I would love to able to control my

atmosphere and the phenomena that lies in between.

If I had control over the world my average day would

be better than a king's. Sometimes I imagine myself

being a prince of the universe with my own element

to control. How beautiful would life be if I was above

PROVERBS OF A TROUBLED SOUL
failure? If I never had to wait would I appreciate

my supremacy? Humility would be in my

actions there would be no need for practice. These

thoughts are compelling but thank God he's the only

being that has control. What do I really know about

control anyway God has existed since before time?

My 29 years of knowledge mocks his majesty and

wisdom. God routinely makes sure his creatures have

substance that dwell in the earth, in the sea, and

on the land above. Why does man desire to have

control and it's something we cannot handle?

Mankind wasn't meant to have control because our

thoughts are too scrambled.

Psalm 139:6
Such knowledge it is too wonderful for me; it is too
high, I cannot attain to it.

"Rejected"

PROVERBS OF A TROUBLED SOUL
Being rejected happens to everybody but it

happens more to people the Lord calls to do great

things. Walking with the lord is never easy but when

we complain it shrinks our space and dreams. I've

found a way for rejection not to kill our joy. I go to

the sacred place in mind where I hid as a boy. In this

sacred place I talk God and I ask him the answers to

the questions that plague mankind. If it wasn't for my

mind's sacred place I would surely lose my mind.

I would die a death of the spirit and I would walk the

earth as one that doesn't know the Lord's grace. I pray

that the Lord will continue to give me unshakable

faith. The rejection of my peers and family members

only makes my spirit strong. Though it's hard when

we're going through it we can make it if we just hold

on. All that I am I owe to rejection it's often a

PROVERBS OF A TROUBLED SOUL

blessing to be alone. I thank everybody who rejected

me you made my faith hard as stone.

John 15:20

Remember the word that I said to you. A servant is not greater than his master. If they persecuted me they will also persecute you.

"New Things"

New things bring new challenges but I'm so ready for

a change. I'm ready for the new friends the Lord

promised to bring into our lives. I'm so ready to say

out with the old and in the with the new. I've been

suffering from the same old things for years now but

most people never knew. It's my time to reap a good

harvest for the good seeds I've planted over the years.

2014 marks the 7th year of my decision to

follow Christ. I've been through hell I'm still going

through hell but I'm never giving up. I may never

PROVERBS OF A TROUBLED SOUL
understand why so much has happened to me in my

life. The trials and tribulations I've had to endure

should have made me bitter and hate the way of

God. Now I understand what it is to struggle and I

don't have anything without God. I'm so ready for

new things so those new opportunities are the ones I

will pursue. The old things of my life are passed away

it's time for the new.

Isaiah 43:19-20
Behold I will do a new thing; now it shall spring
forth; shall ye not know it? I will even make a way in
the wilderness, and rivers in the desert. The beast of
the field shall honor me, the dragons and the owls:
because I give waters in the wilderness and rivers in
the desert, to give to my people, my chosen.

"Love I Found You"

The joy I feel I can't express with words my heart

rejoices at the sound of your name. You are my

helper and my friend I plan to live happy with you

until the end. You took your time with me when I was down and I promise to take my time with you. How good is it that I've finally found you? You lift me up when I'm down you make me feel high when I'm low. I thought a love like you didn't exist but I just didn't know. Having you as my wife is an honor and a privilege I love you more every day. I'm going to do my part to keep us happy my actions will show the way. Many men are afraid to take a chance on love but the reward is much greater than the risk. Love how you changed my heart is a miracle and you sealed it with a kiss. My love I've finally found you it doesn't get better than this.

Ephesians 5:25
Husbands love your wives even also as Christ also loved the church and gave himself for it.